Verrado Heritage Elementary School
20895 W. Hamilton Street
Buckeye, AZ 85396

ARE BOWLING BALLS BULLIES?

Learning About Forces and Motion with THE GARBAGE GANG

by Thomas Kingsley Troupe

illustrated by Derek Toye

PICTURE WINDOW BOOKS
a capstone imprint

MEET THE GARBAGE GANG:

SAM HAMMWICH

Sam is a once-delicious sandwich that has a bit of lettuce and tomato. He is usually crabby and a bit of a loudmouth.

GORDY

Gordy is a small rhino who wears an eyepatch even though he doesn't need one. He lives in the city dump. His friends don't visit him in the smelly dump, so Gordy created his own friends—the Garbage Gang!

SOGGY

Soggy is a stuffed bear from a carnival game. She fell into a puddle of dumpster juice and has never been the same.

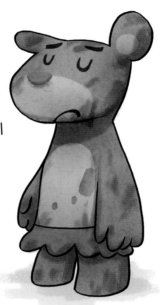

RICK

Rick is a brick. He is terrified of bugs, especially bees, which is odd . . . since he's a brick.

CANN-DEE

Cann-Dee is a robot made of aluminum cans. She can pull random facts out of thin air.

MR. FRIGID

Mr. Frigid is a huge refrigerator that sprouted arms and legs. He doesn't say much, but he's super strong.

3

Glossary

collide—the action of two things striking each other

energy—the ability to do work, such as moving things or giving heat or light

force—a push or pull that changes the movement of an object

frame—in bowling, two throws by one person; if the person gets a strike on the first throw, the frame is over

galaxy—a large group of stars and planets

gravity—force that pulls objects together

magnetic—having the attractive properties of a magnet

predict—to say what you think will happen in the future

strike—in bowling, knocking down all of the pins in one throw

You're looking up words? That's one smart move, kid!

Read More

Kessler, Colleen. *A Project Guide to Forces and Motion.* Physical Science Projects for Kids. Hockessin, Del.: Mitchell Lane Publishers, 2012.

Royston, Angela. *Forces and Motion.* Essential Physical Science. Chicago.: Capstone Heinemann Library, 2014.

Weakland, Mark. *DO-4U the Robot Experiences Forces and Motion.* In the Science Lab. North Mankato, Minn.: Picture Window Books, 2012.

Incoming data suggests that books are a force to be reckoned with.

Critical Thinking Using the Common Core

1. Name two kinds of forces that can place an object in motion.
   (Key Ideas and Details)

2. What is gravity? How does gravity act on objects in motion? How does it act on you?
   (Integration of Knowedge and Ideas)

Index

Internet Sites

FactHound offers a safe, fun way to find Internet sites related to this book. All of the sites on FactHound have been researched by our staff.

Here's all you do:

Visit www.facthound.com

Type in this code: 9781479570577

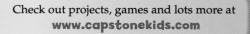

Super-cool stuff! Check out projects, games and lots more at www.capstonekids.com

Thanks to our advisers for their expertise, research, and advice:
Paul Ohmann, PhD, Associate Professor of Physics
University of St. Thomas

Editor: Shelly Lyons
Designer: Aruna Rangarajan
Creative Director: Nathan Gassman
Production Specialist: Morgan Walters
The illustrations in this book were created digitally
Picture Window Books are published by Capstone,
1710 Roe Crest Drive, North Mankato, Minnesota 56003
www.capstonepub.com

Library of Congress Cataloging-in-Publication Data
Troupe, Thomas Kingsley, author.
Are bowling balls bullies? : learning about forces and motion with the Garbage Gang / by Thomas Kingsley Troupe.
pages cm—(Nonfiction picture books. The Garbage Gang's super science questions)
Includes bibliographical references and index.
Summary: "Humorous text and characters help teach kids about forces and motion" — Provided by publisher.
Audience: 5-7.
Audience: K to 3.
ISBN 978-1-4795-7057-7 (library binding)
ISBN 978-1-4795-7067-6 (eBook PDF)
1. Force and energy—Juvenile literature. 2. Motion—Juvenile literature. I. Title. II. Series: Troupe, Thomas Kingsley. Nonfiction picture books. Garbage Gang's super science questions.
QC73.4.T76 2016
531'.6—dc23   2014049605

Printed in the United States of America in North Mankato, Minnesota.
032015   008823CGF15

Look for all the books in the series:

More books! Are you kidding me? This is the best news since sliced bread!

ARE BOWLING BALLS BULLIES? learning about Forces and Motion with **THE GARBAGE GANG**

DO ANTS GET LOST? learning about Animal Communication with **THE GARBAGE GANG**

DO BEES POOP? learning about Living and Nonliving Things with **THE GARBAGE GANG**

DO PLANTS HAVE HEADS? learning about Plant Parts with **THE GARBAGE GANG**

WHAT'S WITH THE LONG NAPS, BEARS? learning about Hibernation with **THE GARBAGE GANG**

WHY DO DEAD FISH FLOAT? learning about Matter with **THE GARBAGE GANG**

WHY DOES MY BODY MAKE BUBBLES? learning about the Digestive System with **THE GARBAGE GANG**

YOU CALL THAT A NOSE? learning about Human Senses with **THE GARBAGE GANG**

Seriously?